SEA-LIGHT

Sea-light

Dinah Hawken

TE HERENGA WAKA
UNIVERSITY PRESS

Te Herenga Waka University Press
PO Box 600, Wellington
New Zealand
teherengawakapress.co.nz

Te Herenga Waka University Press
was formerly Victoria University Press.

A catalogue record is available from the
National Library of New Zealand.

ISBN 9781776564279

Printed by Ligare, Auckland

for Bill, again

Contents

Perhaps peace means creating
so compelling a story of possibility and wellbeing
that people wander out of their bunkers,
put down their weapons and come over.

—*Rebecca Solnit*

Train of thought

I thought of vitality,
I thought of course of a spring.

I thought of the *give* inherent
in the abiding nature of things.

I thought of the curve of a hammock
between amenable trees.

I thought of the lake beyond it
calm and inwardly fluent

and then I was thinking of you.
You appeared out of the water

like a saint appearing from nowhere
as bright as a shining cuckoo

then dripping you stood in the doorway
as delighted by friendship as water

and beaming welcomed us in.

The girl on the train

I was facing her. I could see the whole performance.
The older couple in front had tittered and I looked up
to see her with the brush in her hand.
It was off-peak: we three the only ones facing her way.
She slipped the brush into the foundation
and began, via a small mirror, to attend
to her face with light, confident strokes.
My first thought was 'God, 20-year-olds,
where has feminism gone?'
but as I watched the way she worked
on her brow, cheekbones, cheeks, chin and neck
with the swift intuition of an artist in a studio
all the way from Paekākāriki to Pukerua Bay
my mind changed. I was halfway through
No Great Mischief but it stayed in my bag.
I knew the pleasure of absorption.
I knew intent when I saw it.

But why was her work taking so long?
Perhaps she is obsessive? I thought. Compulsive?
And this ritual keeps her going, keeps her steady
keeps her feeling sane?

From Pukerua Bay to Porirua she worked on her eyes.
A muted palette, with a smaller brush that she moved
with swift, definite gestures from one
set of lashes to the other, her wrist turning

from back to front again and again. Perhaps,
I thought, she is just attention-seeking,
making public, as we do on Facebook,
what would've once been private. But she seemed
unaware of us. Audience was not on her mind.

I know, I thought, she's a drama student, late
out of bed and preparing for a show.
After Porirua she began on her mouth.
Her strokes were small, vertical, and the colour,
like her nails, bright pink. Ah, I thought, that's it
she's a trainee make-up artist practising
on her own face. Perhaps she has an exam?

It was just after Tawa the deodorant appeared.
She pulled out her round-necked top – first on one side
then the other – and concentrated on each armpit
for an unusual length of time. Then I think I clicked.
This was train theatre. Mime. She was playing a role.
We *were* the audience after all. She was making up
the girl on the train to present her to us,
letting us face up to her as she made up her face.
The deodorant was the mischief, the high point,
and the work on the fingernails all the way to Wellington
with her head down and on one side
was the denouement timed beautifully to the end.

Drama

The lake is grey and speechless, in a state
of glimmer and rarely seen light.

Don't disturb it with wishful thinking,
it has *become* wishful thinking.

Think of dreaming, drowning, sleep.
Or just don't think.

A coot, up and over, has gone inside it
barely leaving a trace.

Will I ever learn to let it be, this graceful,
windless, windowless lake?

The sea

The sea is coming straight for us
line after line like an old-fashioned army.

We are looking down to check we are loved
then looking down again to look something up.

'What is a killer robot?' we ask.
'Cold-blooded slaughter' is the answer,

'they're doing it just because they can,
they want to see where it will go.'

★

Where will it go?

★

Without a technical bone
in its immense body

the sea is a security alert,
a crowd in agitation,

an expert in erosion.
The sea is a weight

at the back of our distraction,
it is the sea we are filling up

with acid, the sea that floats
and feeds us coming in

Self-talk of a stern nature

How can you hope to glow or glare,
half-buried in habit, depletion
and winter light?

All flights are over.
You'll have to live
closer to the bone.

The truth is subsidence.

So fall open like an old book in idle hands.
Display yourself on both sides like a single page.

Or look in on Room 2, where the kids
are low to the ground and each
body is occupied by an intent soul.

Try reclamation. Be like the moon
and stand around shamelessly
in borrowed light.

Haze

Some like to get to the bottom of things.
Right down into the dry valleys
with a drill (and a thrill) beneath them.

Some like to live along at eye level
where things like a child or a leaf
are touchable and whole

and nobody cares what they are made of
or where they have come from
because they are here.

Mystery lives round the edges
of things and although the midwife
has two hands, the dragonfly two eyes

and there are two incredible hemispheres,
mystery comes in the odd numbers
with no intention to be clear.

Some see it as select company

or an over-the-top view
like this one from the fore-deck,
where sea-light surrounds the island

as fantasy surrounds reality
and makes a third thing, beauty,
in the evening, from the sea

Body talk

When I was an upstart
my older brother sat on my stomach
held my skinny arms down with his grass-stained knees
and tapped on my boy/girl chest.

The left side of my chest, now breastless and scarred,
reminds me of that girl with barber-cut hair and a mind
that strayed away from home.
Her chest is flat and free. She is running through
damp grass with bare feet at full speed.

Once, playing girls versus boys on a hillside,
I was held down and out like a star
by four big boys in whom something cruel
had begun to turn and sometimes,
from somewhere, a pocket knife appears,
is opened slowly, and glints.

When I was seventy and
the biopsy needle approached
my exposed breast I was asked
to put my arms above my head in surrender.
My whole body contracted in allegiance
to the girl who lives inside me
with a memory of terror.

Now when I wear the breast-form over my scar
I remember that I have been a woman
with two firm loveable breasts. I loved them both.
I loved the seductive way they emptied their milk
and spread contentment all round.

I hope now that my right breast
will be here to know the full story.
While it loosens and softens with age
the left side of my chest
will bear its long scar of commemoration;
from girl to woman, from woman to old woman,
from go, to glow, to woe.

Sticks and stones

No guns.
There are no guns.

No missiles.
No bombs.
No drones.

★

There are sticks and stones.

★

The military man is thinking hard.
His right hand is under his strong chin.

The thoughtful woman is on her feet,
she has raised her deep voice:

a voice with the steel of a gun barrel,
with the roots of the tree of life
and the thrust of a human heart:

no more killing,

no more guns.

★

The military man is thinking hard.
His right hand is under his strong chin.

He is thinking about arms.
The small arms of his children, the long arm
of his father and the longer arm of the law.

He is thinking about size and length and distance.

The distance of a hand from a head and a heart.

He is bending forward into his own thinking
as if it is a small pool at the edge
of a wild and scenic river.

★

Offstage the day-to-day woman
has a child on her back
and a basket in her hands.

She is thinking about rice.
She is thinking about fever.
She is thinking about rain.

Offstage there is corporate uproar
dying down and corporate uproar
fuelling the ashes.

★

The military man asks, 'What next?'
The day-to-day man makes ends meet.

They both see the trust
in the eyes of a child.

The thoughtful woman
is on her feet.

She sees the distance
between a child and a man.

★

Between a child and a man

lenity and cruelty
play for a kingdom.

Today the sea

is predictable – gentle and tidy.

No demands, no clamour
but infinite glamour.

Snow

I carry my declining body and loose mind
into the snow.

Ahead, two nuns – their calm faces
haloed by light – on the expanse of snow.

They push towards a large barn,
the only shelter in that field of snow.

The righteous won't follow them.
They are blinded by snow.

The obedient are cowered
by the open mind – of snow.

The pure and the timid do not like to break the crust
on the surface of snow.

The two nuns are laughing. Freedom
lifts their black wings in the totality of snow.

A small woman returning in a blue urn

I lost my sister
and I found her ashes.

I know she is lighter
I know she has lightened

★

Take her, my nephew said,
as if it was urgent.
So I did. I held her.
I held the urgency
and the urn.

From a small woman
has come three grown men.

★

She was safe in the urn
as I was safe in her house,
the one on stilts amongst palms
that she loved as if her life
in the end
depended on it.

She depended on its beauty
as she depended on the love
that urged us up the outdoor stairs into her room.

*

I held the urn against me
as if my sister was unborn
and walked with her
on the closed-in verandah
of her last worldly home.

Everything surprised me.
My sister was in pieces.
She was at our disposal.

I turned into a kuia
and filled the house
with the echo
and groundswell of grief.

We knew by then
that from a small woman
can come a tall order.

She'd been giving us a way to live
while she was dying:

acceptance, courage, faith,
love for one another,
the fine, hard-earned story.

★

The photograph of a grandchild
and some small stones
were what she held on to
while she was dying.

She was letting *us* let *her*
turn light and boundless

so that a smile of completion
could fall and truly settle
on her human face

Growth

A man came upon a redwood tree
and knew without thinking
what it means to be vertical.

Knowing what is vertical
gave the man height
and height gave him an overview.

Now he could see the island
surrounded by sea-light and knew
that in fact we are blessed.

At home – in his own garden –
he stood under the pōhutukawa tree
and saw the advantage of branching.

He saw the beauty of branching:
the red flowers among pale leaves
open, welcoming bees.

When the red spilt onto the ground
he waded through it learning
the nature of a soft resistance.

He joined the resistance, the one
under the country repairing the damage.
Code words: seeds, waiting, trees.

The sea

is full of ordinary conversation.
Incessant. Like a radio, like a friend.
A presenter who will never leave
a lull that you can enter.

Where is the quiet
between the breaking and
the broken or between
the broken ones themselves?

When will the sea
– as it sometimes does –
become a silent partner?

Listing

I'm a small tower of dubious stability.

I'm a listed building.

Loss of bone, loss of balance, loss of speed, loss of sight,
loss of restraint, loss of muscle, loss of memory, loss of
smell, loss of hearing, loss of words

★

I wish you'd recognise me in the street.
I'm braver you could say
than ever.

I'm a sinking ship,
soon to falter and list.

★

Come closer so I can see who you are.

Don't you see that you are truly
unrepeatable and everything
you have ever done is still detectable.
Even your first steps:

I can see your small hand
on the bed and the rest of you

about to give in and let go – to waver –
and take off. I can see you falling
again and again without failing

because your spirit is in the window
of a small tower and
is of a questing nature

Leaving Hauparu Bay

Day 1

Between the roar of trucks, the roar of cars,
effortless silence.

A shag dries its wings on the jetty, tree ferns stand out
in the bush.

The lake wants nothing. Not even to be seen or heard.

Between trucks, between cars – in the cracks
of productivity –

a scene of never-lasting beauty, an arena of fragile quiet.

Day 2

So much silver spreading towards us the lake looks faint.

Silver with no economic weight!

Given its depth the lake might save us   make us bold

like swans   black on silver   with a touch of red

disarmed   disarming   gliding on

Day 3

I'm here at lake-level with washed-up leaves:

on the verge, with feet in the pumicey sand.

There's a post in the water. The last post.

With a faint sigh when it touches the shore

the lake is asking why I am leaving

when beside it, and in it, I seem to belong.

Day 4

Mind   lake   planet   everything moody.

Except perhaps the land   the land that raised us.

Natives and exotics sway together in the lively bay,

the clouds in innocuous pieces, the lake

in miniature waves, the waves about to go haywire.

Day 5

Earth is the understory, tree ferns the overstory,

the lake the story itself. With an eruptive beginning

ecstatic days   and an unknown end

the lake and the land

meet at the place   where after fifty years

I must leave them.

Chloe

There is a handgun
on a small side-table
beside an armchair.

There is no one in the room.

It is a still life.

*

The gun is loaded
but lying as if extinct.

Beside it lies
a small
handed-down book.

*

Some of the hands
have been old hands:

the old fingertips
on the thin thighs

spread out like suns
but almost weeping.

What have they lived for?

★

Outside,
within earshot,

is the rough, high-spirited
play of children.

★

The gun hears nothing
and has no recall

but it is honoured. The book
has been lifted up

absorbed

and placed carefully down.

★

On the mantelpiece
is the photograph

of a man who looks well
but is dying.

He holds his first grandchild
Chloe
gently in his hands.

Her small head
rests on his upper arm.

★

The wide doors of the room are open
as if all adults
have left the world

as if they have left the constraints
that a room can bestow

as if they are leaving the past,
and leaving the children,

as if all they can see
and all they hope for
is unfettered freedom.

The sea

The sea is coming in friendship
with deep breathing and
an offering of small shells.

I love you like this, Pacific,
when you come bearing your name
and display
the full and final extent
of your self-possession.

Up, up, up they go

I wish they would leave the moon alone.

They know who they are.

They say it's for mankind.

★

I wish I had three wishes.

★

I wish they would leave the moon alone.

I wish they'd fall to Earth and saunter.

I wish they'd look down upon
the faces of their children:

such open, earthly, moonlit faces.

Supremacy

Welcome to the gun club.
Welcome to its glorious noise.
Welcome to the jetski and the chainsaw.
Welcome to a cracking speed.
Welcome to one side,
or the other, to the thrill
of competition, the thrust of division.

And welcome to a world within the world
where one side of a wound tends to seek the other;
where, if you cut a ngaio branch it's inclined
to come back laughing, and where water
even of the quietest kind
gashed open by a speedboat
simply reconvenes.

Uncertainty

There is a lull in the fighting.
The lull is like a lake,
its bed once a volcano.

How do we know
exactly what to do?

Some are mesmerised.
Others dive into it,
total immersion.

Some of us stand
on the bare edge,
on the defensive. Afraid
of a state we've been
breathing so long for.

The sea

The sea is coming out of the haze
with a smooth insistence.

It's as if it is having an idea.
An idea it will certainly fulfil.

Faith

Here is a white mask.
You will need it to get around the city.

Here are your waders
and your fireproof vests.

While colour leaches from the world
you will well up with sorrow.

When coral fades and the sea rises
you will take life above the waterline

and extract from the tolerant earth
insane amounts of faith.

Think of saris lifting like wildfire.
And cows that were turned into gods.

Think silk, spice and sailing ship.
Enter a temple and pray for a temperate rain.

Leaving home

You head off into the wild
as if you are wild

a seed singling itself out
taking to air
and settling for fertile ground

★

On a round day like this one
be open, directionless

don't be afraid
there are so many stones
to choose from   and hold

★

When you see clarity
you'll want to slip into it:
into its pure, riverine beauty

and here's a little lift

to your mid-back
where the wings once were

★

Sometimes you will cry into your pillow
like a child and months later
someone will come towards you
carrying a dozen peonies

Remember the grieving woman
has fingers of sunlight
along her curved spine

★

Self is a soft word, like loft and lift

it is best seen in a soft light

Doing the numbers

1

Most fisherman don't want to collapse
the fish stocks. Not quickly anyway.
Most farmers don't want to pollute
rivers and streams. Not gravely anyway.
Growers don't want to ruin the soil.
There must be engineers who hate to see
wetlands drained and trees overturned.
They don't want flooding or erosion.
There could be mining magnates
who care deeply for the seabed.
For reefs and their creatures.

2

It's harder to see what leaders want.
They seem to snag like bycatch
on what they think the above want,
while − from well above the above −
it's clear that no one wants to drown
in sliding mud, collapse on a road
in a heatwave, or be entangled
in the debris and rage of a flood.
No one wants to live through famine
or fire then happen to die with a child
in his arms, caught in a war over water.

You never know

1

I used to think 'pass away'
was a euphemism,
a kind of cowering,
but since my sister died
I believe in pass
and I believe in away

2

I could roll up
in silence
like one of the lily's
orange petals, detached now
from the others
who have also fallen

and simply lie there

curling and slowly drying
like my sister, a herald, a harbinger,
a small tongue of fire

3

Later I might turn
into the fine dust
that surprised me this morning
falling out of an old book
onto my thigh, leaving
– in the bottom right-hand corner
of the fragile pages –
a tracery of fine lines
sparing the text and
the worm long gone

The sea

is putting on a tremendous show
of white fire and invigoration.

As far as the eye can see, lines of swell are rising
and eight are breaking.

They're an irrefutable argument.
Backed by centuries of evidence.

As the sun goes down and the seaspray flies
John is out there on his board while we,

watching, are nervous and enthralled.
And the argument is this: the ocean is greater

than the human race; it is warming, rising
and vomiting our plastic back.

It is saner than our submarines,
fish are its protected species,

seabirds are its flights of fancy
and for us it has no name.

Mercy

Take her to the room of tiny writing.
She is scaling down, diminishing.

Leave her there unattended
and she'll ingest the tiny writing – one stalk,
one branch, one root, one leaf at a time.

If you don't leave her there
you'll have a witch on your hands,
a tiny one in your left palm
testing a sword.

She has practised all her life to release
the chi of tiny writing and to come out
spirited in the palm of a merciful hand.

Oceania

The steel-blue swell is even-minded and
        like winter   vigorous and clean.

From the beginning I have been waiting
for a day filled with night.

What I wish for you
        in the building up and breaking down
        in the tyranny of competition
        in a twilight of haze and confluence

is the medieval word *well*. You are a well-spring.
And its vessel.

★

Will you bend to the sun in the bend of the river?

★

I wish you well.

I wish you the silence of a girl with a brush in her hand.
I wish you the virtuous silence of standing out
and the faithful silence of fitting in.

I wish you faith in your own firm voice and I wish
for a measured rise and fall of oceanic water.

The tiny spider

'We will have to tackle ourselves
down to the ground
to hold back global warning'
I had written in my journal
when a tiny spider appeared,
exploring the word 'we'
and running down the page to stop
at 'exploitative corporations'.
While I watched, the tiny spider
crawled off the page
onto my leafy patterned pants
and became hard to detect.
Would it crawl up under my shirt
onto my bare skin? Why was I afraid?

I manoeuvred it onto the memorial card
for Miriam's Requiem Mass
and the tiny spider crawled without a footprint
onto Miriam's lively eyes
and across her mischievous face.

I took the card outside, tilting it
to encourage the spider onto a red petunia petal.
Onto a green leaf? But it spun a thread of web,
dropped into the air
and attached itself to a strand of native grass.

We were no longer connected.
Well that's not true: we now have a lasting relationship.
The spider drew attention to the word
'we' and in turn I remembered that arachnids
are on the brink of extinction. The spider re-called me
to Miriam's face, her laugh and love of life
and I saw they had not been lost. Together, all together
we turned a journal entry about severe weather
into an elegy for the living and the dead,
for creatures great and small
and the quiet waters by.

After that I won't say a word to anyone

There will be silence.
I will be seen but not heard.

When the time comes
the quiet word we've had together
will be written all over our faces – hovering
in the eloquence of silence.

Before that I'd like to put this in writing:
silence is not deathly,
it is not deafening.

While the sea and the traffic roars
your tongue can retreat to the roof
of your mouth and live quietly

out of reach, out of trouble
and re-emerge in the buoyancy

of silence

Notes and acknowledgements

The epigraph (p. 9) is a found poem. It comes from an essay I read in the *Guardian Weekly* (Nov. 4, 2018), by Rebecca Solnit: 'The American Civil War didn't end. And Trump is a confederate president'. I have changed the wording minimally.
theguardian.com/commentisfree/2018/nov/04/ the-american-civil-war-didnt-end-and-trump-is-a-confederate-president

The last two lines of 'Sticks and stones' (p. 22) are borrowed from Shakespeare's *Henry V*, Act 3, scene 6. The full quote is: 'When lenity and cruelty play for a kingdom, the gentlest gamester is the soonest winner.'

In 'Oceania' (p. 53), the words 'virtuous' and 'faithful' came to mind from the title of Louise Glück's book of poetry, *Faithful and Virtuous Night* (Farrar, Straus & Giroux, 2014).

'Train of thought' (p. 11) has previously appeared on Paula Green's website *Poetry Shelf*, and 'Haze' (p. 18) in the Irish literary magazine *Cyphers*. With thanks to the editors.